George Gordon Meade

Union General

Colonial Leaders

Lord Baltimore
English Politician and Colonist

Benjamin Banneker
American Mathematician and Astronomer

Sir William Berkeley
Governor of Virginia

William Bradford
Governor of Plymouth Colony

Jonathan Edwards
Colonial Religious Leader

Benjamin Franklin
American Statesman, Scientist, and Writer

Anne Hutchinson
Religious Leader

Cotton Mather
Author, Clergyman, and Scholar

Increase Mather
Clergyman and Scholar

James Oglethorpe
Humanitarian and Soldier

William Penn
Founder of Democracy

Sir Walter Raleigh
English Explorer and Author

Caesar Rodney
American Patriot

John Smith
English Explorer and Colonist

Miles Standish
Plymouth Colony Leader

Peter Stuyvesant
Dutch Military Leader

George Whitefield
Clergyman and Scholar

Roger Williams
Founder of Rhode Island

John Winthrop
Politician and Statesman

John Peter Zenger
Free Press Advocate

Revolutionary War Leaders

John Adams
Second U.S. President

Samuel Adams
Patriot

Ethan Allen
Revolutionary Hero

Benedict Arnold
Traitor to the Cause

John Burgoyne
British General

George Rogers Clark
American General

Lord Cornwallis
British General

Thomas Gage
British General

King George III
English Monarch

Nathanael Greene
Military Leader

Nathan Hale
Revolutionary Hero

Alexander Hamilton
First U.S. Secretary of the Treasury

John Hancock
President of the Continental Congress

Patrick Henry
American Statesman and Speaker

William Howe
British General

John Jay
First Chief Justice of the Supreme Court

Thomas Jefferson
Author of the Declaration of Independence

John Paul Jones
Father of the U.S. Navy

Thaddeus Kosciuszko
Polish General and Patriot

Lafayette
French Freedom Fighter

James Madison
Father of the Constitution

Francis Marion
The Swamp Fox

James Monroe
American Statesman

Thomas Paine
Political Writer

Molly Pitcher
Heroine

Paul Revere
American Patriot

Betsy Ross
American Patriot

Baron Von Steuben
American General

George Washington
First U.S. President

Anthony Wayne
American General

Famous Figures of the Civil War Era

John Brown
Abolitionist

Jefferson Davis
Confederate President

Frederick Douglass
Abolitionist and Author

Stephen A. Douglas
Champion of the Union

David Farragut
Union Admiral

Ulysses S. Grant
Military Leader and President

Stonewall Jackson
Confederate General

Joseph E. Johnston
Confederate General

Robert E. Lee
Confederate General

Abraham Lincoln
Civil War President

George Gordon Meade
Union General

George McClellan
Union General

William Henry Seward
Senator and Statesman

Philip Sheridan
Union General

William Sherman
Union General

Edwin Stanton
Secretary of War

Harriet Beecher Stowe
Author of Uncle Tom's Cabin

James Ewell Brown Stuart
Confederate General

Sojourner Truth
Abolitionist, Suffragist, and Preacher

Harriet Tubman
Leader of the Underground Railroad

Famous Figures of the Civil War Era

George Gordon Meade

Union General

Bruce Adelson

Arthur M. Schlesinger, jr.
Senior Consulting Editor

Chelsea House Publishers

Philadelphia

CHELSEA HOUSE PUBLISHERS
Editor-in-Chief Sally Cheney
Director of Production Kim Shinners
Production Manager Pamela Loos
Art Director Sara Davis
Production Editor Diann Grasse

Staff for *GEORGE GORDON MEADE*
Editor Sally Cheney
Associate Art Director Takeshi Takahashi
Series Design Keith Trego
Layout by D&G Limited, LLC

The Chelsea House World Wide Web address is
http://www.chelseahouse.com

First Printing
1 3 5 7 9 8 6 4 2

Library of Congress Cataloging-in-Publication Data

Adelson, Bruce.
    George Meade : Union general / Bruce Adelson.
        p. cm. — (Famous figures of the Civil War era)
    Includes bibliographical references and index.
    ISBN 0-7910-6410-7 (alk. paper) — ISBN 0-7910-6411-5 (pbk. :
    alk. paper)
      1. Meade, George Gordon, 1815-1872—Juvenile literature.
    2. Generals—United States—Biography—Juvenile literature. 3.
    United States. Army—Biography—Juvenile literature. 4. United
    States—History—Civil War, 1861-1865—Campaigns—Juvenile
    literature. [1. Meade, George Gordon, 1815-1872. 2. Generals.
    3. United
    States—History—Civil War, 1861-1865.] I. Title. II. Series.

    E467.1.M38 A34 2001
    973.7'349'092—dc21
    [B]   2001028766

Publisher's Note: In Colonial, Revolutionary War, and Civil War Era America, there were no standard rules for spelling, punctuation, capitalization, or grammar. Some of the quotations that appear in the Colonial Leaders, Revolutionary War Leaders, and Famous Figures of the Civil War Era series come from original documents and letters written during this time in history. Original quotations reflect writing inconsistencies of the period.

Contents

George Gordon Meade was born on December 31, 1815, in Cadiz, Spain, while his father worked there as a business-man and naval agent for the U.S. government.

A Reluctant Soldier

As a Union army general during the Civil War, George Gordon Meade became famous for winning the Battle of Gettysburg, probably the most important battle of the whole war. But earlier in his life, no one suspected that George Meade would one day help save his country.

George was born on December 31, 1815, in Cadiz, Spain. His father, Richard Meade, worked as a businessman and naval agent for the U.S. government in Spain. As a naval agent, Richard Meade arranged to send products made in Spain to the United States, and American products to Spain on American ships.

Richard Meade was in jail on the day his son George was born. The Spanish police arrested him after he had a business dispute with the King of Spain.

George's mother, Margaret Meade, tried to have her husband released from prison, but she was unsuccessful. Worried about her and George's safety, she arranged in 1817 for them to return by ship to the United States. At that time, young George was only about one and a half years old.

After arriving in the United States, Margaret and her son settled in Philadelphia, Pennsylvania, where Margaret continued trying to free her husband from the Spanish prison. Finally, in 1818, good news came. Richard was out of jail and on his way home to the United States. When he arrived, he moved the Meade family to Washington, D.C., where he planned to start a business and raise his son.

George's parents sent him to private school when he was about six years old. As a wealthy businessman, his father could send George to well-known and expensive schools. But Richard Meade's success did not last. When George was about 10 years old, his father's business began to fail. Soon, the Meades were running out of money.

Richard Meade died in 1827, when George was 12. Without much money, Margaret Meade knew she could not pay for George's private school education anymore. She looked for a school that she could afford.

Through his business dealings as a U.S. naval agent, Richard Meade had met many important people. Margaret Meade asked some of them for help in finding a school for George. With their assistance, she was able to obtain an appointment for her son to the United States Military Academy in West Point, New York. The academy, known as West Point, is a college where students are trained to be officers in the U.S. Army. In 1831, when he was almost 16 years old, George Meade left home and entered West Point.

George had never said he was interested in becoming a soldier. But he wanted to follow his mother's wishes. He struggled with some of his classes at his new school, but he worked hard and graduated in 1835.

When he graduated, 20-year-old George Meade was made a second lieutenant in the U.S. Army. The army assigned him to an artillery unit in Florida, where the United States was fighting the **Seminole War** against a tribe of Native Americans known as Seminoles.

In January 1836, Lieutenant Meade arrived in Tampa, Florida. He had never before been in a place as hot and humid as Florida, and soon after his arrival, George became sick from the climate. His illness prevented him from fighting in the Seminole War, so he was soon given another job. George Meade was sent to Watertown, Massachusetts, where he worked in the Watertown **Arsenal**, a place where some of the army's guns and ammunition were kept.

George's first post was as a second lieutenant in an artillery unit in Florida. In 1835 the United States was at war there with a tribe of Native Americans known as Seminoles.

At that time, all West Point graduates had to remain in the army for at least one year. In 1836, after George had completed his year of service, he resigned. Being a soldier still did not interest him. Instead, George was determined to find a job that he really liked.

In 1837, George found work as a railroad sur-veyor, making maps of areas where railroads were going to be built. George discovered that he enjoyed being a surveyor. After he left his railroad map job, he found a similar position surveying the Mississippi River and the borders of the state of Maine for the U.S. Army. George was working for the army again, but not as a soldier. He was a civil-ian surveyor and enjoyed his new career.

In 1839, George met Margaretta Sargent, the daughter of a U.S. Congressman. They fell in love and were married in 1840. George and Margaretta Meade had a happy life together until 1842 when George lost his job. That year, Congress passed a law that said only soldiers, not civilians like George Meade, could work as engineers and surveyors for the army. George asked the army to let him be a soldier again so that he could return to his old job and support his wife. The army agreed, making George Meade a second lieutenant of engineers.

The first significant battle of the Mexican-American War was in Palo Alto, where George served the United States as a courier.

Lieutenant Meade was sent back to Maine to complete his mapping project there. After finishing this job, George designed and built lighthouses in Delaware. George didn't mind being a soldier again because he was doing what he enjoyed.

But in 1845, his life changed when tensions developed between the United States and Mexico over Texas. At that time many nations, including the United States, considered Texas to be an independent country. Texas had been a part of Mexico in 1835, but in 1836, Texas won a war of independence against that country.

In 1845, the Mexican government still considered Texas to be part of Mexico. Much of the land that today makes up the western part of the United States, including California and New Mexico, was also then controlled by Mexico.

Shortly after becoming U.S. president in 1845, James K. Polk asked the people of Texas to vote on whether or not they wanted their state to become part of the United States. This angered large numbers of Mexican people. But despite the Mexicans' anger, many Texans wanted to be Americans. On July 4, 1845, the people of Texas voted to become part of the United States.

American soldiers were sent to Texas in August 1845 to protect the newest part of their country.

Lieutenant Meade went to Corpus Christi, Texas, where he joined the staff of General Zachary Taylor.

Over the next few months, the American and Mexican armies prepared for the possibility of war. On April 24, 1846, Mexican General Mariano Arista sent a letter to General Taylor warning him that he would fight the Americans unless they left Texas immediately. The next day, the Mexican army crossed the Rio Grande River, rode into Texas, and attacked. Sixteen American soldiers were killed or wounded in the battle. The Mexican-American War had begun.

Lieutenant Meade participated in the Battle of Palo Alto, the first big battle of the war, as a courier, delivering messages between General Taylor and his officers. The American army won this battle and forced the Mexican army to retreat. The next day, the Americans defeated the Mexicans again at the Battle of Resaca de la Palma. George was also a courier in this battle.

On February 2, 1848, Mexico and the United States signed the Treaty of Guadalupe Hidalgo. This was a peace treaty that ended the Mexican-American War. In the treaty, Mexico agreed to pay the United States $15,000,000. This was an even larger sum of money in 1848 than it is today. Mexico also gave the United States a large amount of land. Today, this land is included in seven states of the United States—Arizona, California, Colorado, Nevada, New Mexico, Texas, and Utah.

On September 21, 1846, Lieutenant Meade led a small group of soldiers up Independence Hill to take over a Mexican fort. In his first battle leading troops against enemy soldiers, George and his men captured the fort. For his bravery, George Meade was promoted to the rank of first lieutenant.

After another year of fighting, the Mexican-American War finally ended on September 14, 1847, when the U.S. army captured Mexico City, the capital of Mexico. The United States had won the war.

After this conflict ended, George was sent back to Washington and was given his old job,

The covers from a series of biographies of Civil War heroes, including George, are shown here.

designing and building lighthouses in Delaware. When he finished this assignment, George traveled back to Florida to design and build lighthouses and breakwaters. Breakwaters, usually made of stone, help save beaches by preventing erosion of sand by the ocean's waves. After finishing his job in Florida, George was sent to Detroit, Michigan, to survey the Great Lakes. In 1856, while in Michigan, George was promoted to the rank of captain.

George Meade was happy with this work. But the army had other plans for him. In 1860 the United States was getting ready for another war. This would be a civil war, with the country breaking apart. Many citizens in the Northern States wanted to abolish, or outlaw, slavery. However, plantation owners in the Southern States needed the cheap labor slavery provided to keep their economy thriving. This issue would divide the Union, with many Southern States seeking to create their own nation, called the Confederate States of America. With such a war, the United States would need all of its sol-diers, including George Meade. In the Civil War, he would have the most important job of his life. George Meade became a general, com-manding soldiers in one of the biggest battles in American history.

Men, women, and children were taken from Africa and brought to the United States. They were then sold to plantation owners in the South. Slaves worked for little or no money in the fields and homes of their owners, and they had no rights or freedoms. This arrangement benefited the plantation owners and was an important part of the Southern economy. Plantation owners could operate their farms with very few expenses.

A Country
Divided

By 1860 the United States was a country divided over the issue of the enslavement of African Americans. Many people in the Northern states opposed slavery and wanted it to be abolished. Many Southerners supported slavery, and did not want Northerners or the government in Washington, D.C., telling them whether or not they could own slaves. Wealthy Southerners bought African Americans and used them to do many things for them, including cooking, cleaning, and farming work, paying them little or no money. These African Americans belonged to their owners and had no freedom.

On February 8, 1861, representatives from seven Southern states met in Montgomery, Alabama. They created a new country, the Confederate States of America. These representatives also wrote a constitution for the new country. This constitution stated that slavery would be permitted everywhere in the Confederate States of America. The first seven Confederate states were Alabama, Florida, Georgia, Louisiana, Mississippi, South Carolina, and Texas. By the end of 1861, four more states seceded from the United States and joined the Confederacy. These states were Arkansas, North Carolina, Tennessee, and Virginia.

As the United States grew, Northerners and Southerners argued about whether slavery should be permitted in the country's new states and territories. This argument had been going on for many years, without addressing what would happen to slavery.

In November 1860, Abraham Lincoln, from the Northern state of Illinois, was elected the country's 16th president. After Lincoln's election, most Southerners decided they did not want to be part of the United States anymore because the new president opposed slavery. One by one, beginning with South Carolina in 1860, the Southern states voted to secede from the

The first battle of the Civil War took place at Fort Sumter when Confederate soldiers attacked and had their first victory in the harbor of Charleston, South Carolina.

United States. This meant that they did not want to be part of the United States anymore, and decided to form a separate nation.

In July 1861 the Confederate states established their capital city in Richmond, Virginia. The states remaining in the United States, called the **Union**, and the Confederate States were angry with each other over slavery, and America was on the verge of war. It was just a matter of time before someone fired the first shot.

On April 12, 1861, the Civil War began when Confederate soldiers fired on Fort Sumter, a fort held by the United States in the harbor of Charleston, South Carolina. After the fort surrendered, the Confederacy had its first victory of the war.

Despite losing Fort Sumter, many people in the North expected the larger, better-equipped Union army to defeat the Confederates easily. In July, a Union army of 35,000 soldiers marched out of Washington, D.C., planning to destroy any Confederate troops they found. But at the First Battle of Bull Run, which is a small creek near the town of Manassas, Virginia, Union soldiers were so badly beaten that they ran from the battlefield back to Washington. After this defeat, the North and South knew the war would not be over anytime soon. They prepared to fight what would turn out to be a long, bloody conflict.

George was a brigadier general in charge of about 10,000 soldiers from Pennsylvania. At the beginning of the war, he spent most of his time with his soldiers, guarding Washington, D.C.

When the war began, George was 46 years old and a captain in the U.S. Army. Like other army officers, George was ready to fight for his country and waited for his first assignment. In August, Pennsylvania Governor Andrew Curtin urged President Lincoln to promote George to the rank of **general**. Lincoln agreed, and George became a brigadier general in command of a **brigade** in the **Division** of Pennsylvania Reserves. This division contained about 10,000 soldiers, all from Pennsylvania.

While several battles were fought in the war's first year, George spent his time with his Pennsylvania soldiers in Washington, D.C., strengthening the defenses of the capital. After spending the winter of 1861–1862 in Washington, George and his division received orders to fight. They traveled south to Virginia where they would try to capture Richmond. Union generals and President Lincoln wanted to end the war quickly and thought they could do so by capturing the Confederacy's capital.

The Army of the Potomac, which had 100,000 Union soldiers, went to Virginia under the command of General George McClellan. This military operation became known as the Peninsula **Campaign** because the Union soldiers who traveled to Virginia by boat had landed on a peninsula east of Richmond and marched toward the capital. A peninsula is a piece of land surrounded on three sides by water.

Although the Union forces outnumbered the Confederates, they could not capture Richmond. Confederate Generals Robert E. Lee and Stonewall Jackson outsmarted General McClellan, and defeated the United States in several battles. Union troops, angry and embarrassed by their defeat, boarded their ships again and retreated to Washington. During the Peninsula Campaign, George fought in his first battle of the war. At the Battle of Glendale, Virginia, on June 30, George was seriously wounded twice. He spent about six weeks in an army hospital recovering from his wounds.

After George's wounds healed, the army sent him back to Virginia, where he rejoined his soldiers. On August 29 and 30, 1862, Union and Confederate armies fought at Bull Run again. The rebels defeated the Union again at what became known as the Second Battle of Bull Run. This was one of the bloodiest fights of the war so far. There were more than 26,000 Union and Confederate casualties. But it was in this battle that U.S. leaders noticed George's military skill.

As most of the Union army retreated, George was ordered to stay behind and prevent the rebels from attacking the fleeing troops. With large numbers of Confederate soldiers charging after their enemy, George placed his men in front of them. His soldiers stopped the Confederate charge and saved the rest of the Union army from destruction. After beating back the rebels, George withdrew his men from the battle, and his unit was one of the last to cross Bull Run Creek on the way back to Washington.

With several battlefield losses in a row, some people in the North worried that the Confederates might win the Civil War. Northerners began to talk about ending the conflict, even if that meant allowing the Confederate States of America to be an independent country. France and Great Britain also talked about helping both sides end the war, leaving two countries, the

United States and Confederate States. Even President Lincoln was worried. After the Second Battle of Bull Run, he told his assistant, John Hay, "Well, John, we are whipped again, I'm afraid." Confident after the Second Battle of Bull Run, Confederate General Lee decided to take his Army of Northern Virginia across the Potomac River and invade Pennsylvania and Maryland. Lee had several reasons for his invasion. He wanted to find new supplies of food and clothing for his soldiers. Lee hoped that a successful invasion could convince Maryland, a neutral state, also called a border state, with many slaves, to join the Confederacy. Lee also believed that another big victory could convince France and Britain to help the Confederacy defeat the Union. If things went well, Lee's army could even threaten to attack nearby Washington, D.C.

On September 9, 1862, as the Confederates marched north, Lee wrote Special Order No. 191 with his plans for the invasion. Somehow, the Confederates lost a copy of this order, which was found by a Union soldier. This soldier gave the order to Union General McClellan who now knew Lee's plans. McClellan prepared for the Confederates, and waited with the Army of the Potomac for Lee at the Maryland town of Sharpsburg, located next to Antietam Creek.

When the Confederates arrived on September 17, McClellan attacked and the Battle of Antietam began. Lee quickly realized he was outnumbered. There were 37,400 Confederates and about 56,000 Union troops. Union attacks against Lee's line succeeded in pushing the Confederates back. George commanded a section of the Union army that was on the right side of the battlefield. Despite heavy Confederate fire, George moved his men forward and Lee's army retreated.

Although George was wounded again, this time in the neck, he did not leave the battle. He continued leading his men, urging them to keep fighting even after they saw their leader hurt by Confederate shellfire. By nightfall, the fighting

Union General McClellan fought General Lee's soldiers at Antietam. In one day of fighting, the Union and the Confederacy each lost over 10,000 soldiers.

stopped. The Battle of Antietam was a Union victory and one of the bloodiest battles of the war, with the Union suffering 12,400 casualties, and the Confederates having lost 10,300 soldiers all in only one day of fighting.

Throughout 1862, Abraham Lincoln waited for a big Union victory to make an important announcement. With the Confederate defeat at Antietam, Lincoln issued the Emancipation Proclamation on January 1, 1863, freeing all slaves in areas in rebellion against the United States or owned by men who were fighting against the United States. African Americans throughout the South rejoiced, knowing that Lincoln considered them to be free people. Confederates became even angrier with Lincoln after the proclamation, saying he was still interfering with their lives. But Lincoln wanted the world to know that the North was fighting the South to end slavery.

The Confederates retreated south, across the Potomac River again and back to Virginia. McClellan stopped Lee's invasion of the North, and George Meade had again impressed military leaders with his skill. But President Lincoln was unhappy with General McClellan. Before the battle, Lincoln ordered McClellan to "Destroy the rebel army, if possible." By not following Lee into Virginia, McClellan failed to smash Lee's army and possibly end the war. Dissatisfied with his commanding general, Lincoln began thinking of a replacement for McClellan. In November, after McClellan again failed to attack Lee, Lincoln fired his general and replaced him with Ambrose Burnside. Also in November, George Meade was recognized for his achievements, and promoted to the rank of major general.

In December, Burnside marched the Army of the Potomac, which included George and more than 120,000 soldiers, toward Richmond. He planned to attack the Confederate capital again.

Hearing about Burnside's invasion of Virginia, General Lee brought his army to Fredericksburg, a town about 45 miles north of Richmond. With 78,000 Confederate soldiers positioned on top of a hill, behind fences and barricades, the Confederates waited for the Union army. On December 13, Burnside decided to attack the Confederates, even though they were in protected positions on top of the hill. It would be hard to defeat the Confederates, but Burnside attacked anyway.

George and his soldiers were on the left of the Union battle line. As the blue uniformed U.S. soldiers advanced up the hill, they were hit by heavy enemy rifle and cannon fire. The Army of the Potomac suffered many casualties that day. Fredericksburg turned out to be another costly defeat for the Union army, with more than 12,500 men killed or wounded.

Even though the Union army was defeated at Fredericksburg, George Meade's men successfully captured more than 300 Confederate prisoners. George's division was even able to advance, while the rest of the Union army retreated, against a portion of the Confederate army that was commanded by General Stonewall Jackson. But without help from other Union troops, George and his men were soon almost surrounded by the enemy. He ordered his men to retreat before being captured. Frustrated that no other soldiers helped his men with their attack, George told another general after the battle, "Did they think my division could whip Lee's whole army?"

After the Battle of Fredericksburg, Lincoln fired General Burnside. He was replaced as

The Army of the Potomac lost the Battle of Fredericksburg, but as the Union retreated, George and his men were able to advance against a portion of the Confederate army. Eventually, George was forced to retreat when he was surrounded by enemy troops.

commander by General Joseph Hooker in January 1863. George was also promoted, and given command of the Fifth Corps, a large part of the Army of the Potomac.

Through the rest of the winter of 1862–1863, both armies watched each other carefully, on

General George Hooker was fired by President Abraham Lincoln after loosing the Battle of Chancellorsville. George Meade was given the job of commander of the Army of the Potomac on June 28, 1863.

opposite sides of the Rappahannock River in Virginia. By spring, General Hooker planned to attack Lee. He ordered George's Fifth Corps, and two other corps, to cross the Rappahannock and Rapidan Rivers, surprise Lee, and attack the rebels. On May 1, 1863, the Union and Confederate armies began fighting near the small town of Chancellorsville. There, more than 190,000 soldiers battled for several bloody days in thick wilderness, with so many trees and branches that the men had trouble seeing any sunlight. By May 6, after suffering more than 17,000 casualties, Hooker pulled his army back across the Rappahannock. But once again, despite bad news for the Union, George Meade and his soldiers fought well.

Another defeat angered President Lincoln almost more than ever before. Many of his advisers felt the Army of the Potomac needed a new commander, again. After the Confederate army crossed the Potomac River and advanced into Maryland and Pennsylvania, Lincoln agreed. The president fired General Hooker, and began the search for another new commander.

George was in command of the 120,000 soldiers of the Army of the Potomac. The army is shown marching through Washington, D.C.

The Battle of Gettysburg

George's superiors thought very highly of him. But George did not want to command the Army of the Potomac. Despite his feelings, many important generals and leaders, including Pennsylvania Governor Darius Couch, recommended to Lincoln that he select George for the job. On June 28, 1863, George Meade accepted President Lincoln's offer to command the army. George Meade now had the biggest job of his life, commanding the Army of the Potomac and more than 120,000 soldiers.

His men knew their new commander very well, even though he had not commanded the army before. George had a reputation for being an excellent and courageous fighter who did not retreat from the enemy. His soldiers knew their commander would give them the chance to fight and defeat the Confederates. They also under-stood that George had a bad temper and angered quickly if people didn't follow orders. His men nicknamed their commander the Snap-ping Turtle because they believed that like a powerful snapping turtle, he would hold onto his enemy until victory.

George had no time to waste. With the South-ern army on the move in Pennsylvania, he needed to get his men ready for what would turn out to be one of the most famous battles in American history.

The Confederate president, Jefferson Davis, and General Robert E. Lee, decided to invade the North again in the spring of 1863. The war was going well for the Confederacy, and Davis and Lee believed they could force the Union to surrender if the Union could be defeated on a

Confederate General Robert E. Lee was a skilled military leader in the U.S. Army before the Civil War began. He left the U.S. Army and fought for the South during the war. Lee would eventually surrender to General Grant to end the war.

Northern battleground. Lee also needed more supplies and food for his soldiers. He knew that there had been very little fighting in Maryland

and Pennsylvania. Both states should have plenty of supplies for his army.

In June 1863, Lee marched his 89,000 troops north from Fredericksburg, across the Potomac River into Maryland and Pennsylvania for the second time in two years.

After capturing York and Chambersburg, Pennsylvania, in late June, Lee met with his generals on June 30 to plan the next move. At that time, Confederate and Union armies were spread out over a large area near Gettysburg, a small town in southern Pennsylvania close to the Maryland border. A small group of Confederate soldiers entered Gettysburg on June 30 in search of shoes and other supplies. They saw some Union troops and quickly retreated. Lee did not want the battle to start too soon.

When he met with his generals, Lee ordered all parts of his army to come together at Cashtown, a small village about eight miles west of Gettysburg. The Confederate generals left the meeting and began to move their troops to Cashtown.

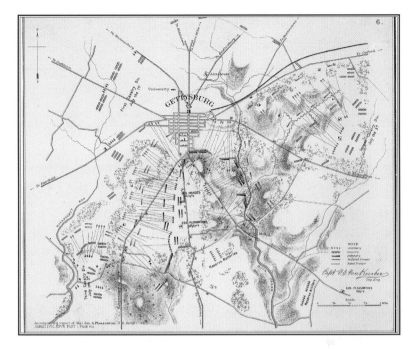

This map of Gettysburg, Pennsylvania, shows the positions of artillery, cavalry, and infantry during the war.

But before this could be done, Union cavalry commanded by General John Buford spotted Confederate infantry led by General Harry Heth marching through Gettysburg. Buford realized he could not wait for the rest of George's army. He had to stop the Confederates himself.

Around 8:00 A.M. on July 1, 1863, at a place called McPherson's Ridge, Buford attacked

Heth's soldiers. Corporal Alphonse Hughes, a Union soldier from New York, is credited with firing the shot that began the Battle of Gettysburg.

Buford's cavalry fought well, although his men were outnumbered. By the end of the day, Buford could not defeat the Confederates. Instead, he withdrew his men from Gettysburg. They took positions just outside of town in several hills, called Cemetery Ridge, Culp's Hill, Little Round Top, and Big Round Top, which surrounded Gettysburg. Rather than chase the retreating Union soldiers, the Confederates stayed in Gettysburg and waited for Lee and the rest of the army. Buford ordered his men to dig holes and build barricades to protect themselves from enemy bullets. He knew that the Confederates could attack at any time. They waited for George and the other Union troops.

By early morning on July 2, the rest of both armies had arrived. There were now more than 160,000 soldiers facing each other at Gettysburg. When the Union army reached Gettysburg,

George found the positions of General Buford's soldiers. This was where George decided to put the rest of his troops. As George looked over the battlefield, he was pleased with what he saw. Buford had done a good job. His soldiers were placed in several strong positions south of town overlooking the Confederate army below them. He felt confident that he was in a good position to win the fight.

But General Lee thought differently. Lee was disappointed that General Heth did not defeat the Union army the day before. He also was unhappy that the Union army held all the hills around Gettysburg. Lee knew that it would be hard to attack uphill during the battle, with the enemy shooting down at his men.

But General Lee still felt confident that his men would defeat the Union, as they had done so many times in the past two years. Early in the morning, he ordered General James Longstreet to attack. But Longstreet disagreed with his commander, believing the Union position was too strong. Longstreet worried that the Confederates would lose if they attacked George's soldiers. By nightfall, Longstreet proved to be correct.

Despite several attacks against the left side of the Union position at Cemetery Ridge, Longstreet failed to push the Union soldiers off the high ground they occupied. While Longstreet attacked the Union troops on the left side of the battlefield, George sent soldiers from the right and center of his position to help soldiers on the left. These **reinforcements** helped defeat Longstreet's men and push them back down the ridge. During Longstreet's charge, the right side of the Union army defeated a second, smaller attack by other troops commanded by Confederate General Ewell. After a second day of fighting, the armies remained in basically the same places they were on July 1.

Lee was in a tough spot. Facing a strong Union army, he could leave Gettysburg, and look for other places to fight. Instead, he decided to attack one last time, sending more than 15,000 soldiers, commanded by General Pickett, toward the center and strongest part of

Confederate General Pickett led his men into battle against Union troops in Gettysburg. Pickett's Charge against the Union troops on Cemetery Ridge failed. The 15,000 Confederates and their 130 cannons could not defeat the powerful Union forces.

the Union army, which was waiting on Cemetery Ridge. Lee still believed his men could defeat the Union in any battle they fought.

Pickett's division of 15,000 men was part of a larger group of soldiers, called a **corps**, commanded by Longstreet. His men were the best rested in the Confederate army since they had not yet fought at Gettysburg. Longstreet again disagreed with General Lee, but he did as he was told. He told Pickett to attack.

But first, Lee ordered Confederate cannons to fire at the Union army on Cemetery Ridge. Around midday, about 130 Confederate cannons began the biggest bombardment ever seen or heard in North America. Cannon ball after cannon ball flew toward the Union position. The noise from the cannon fire was so loud it was heard as far away as Frederick, Maryland, more than 20 miles from the battle.

Finally, the bombardment stopped. Confederate soldiers advanced from a small forest and moved toward the ridge. The 15,000 Confederates marched through an open field to reach their enemy. As they approached the ridge, the Union soldiers began firing at them. This attack, known as Pickett's Charge, became one of the most famous in American history.

In less than an hour, almost 10,000 Confederate soldiers had been killed or wounded by bullets and shells. But the rest of Pickett's men kept marching. One group of Confederates even managed to reach the ridge and push back some Union soldiers. But these Confederates were quickly outnumbered and surrounded.

Soon it was clear that the attack failed, and the surviving members of Pickett's division retreated, moving back to the forest where they began their charge. Lee was wrong. This time, the Union army, commanded by George Meade, defeated the Confederates. The Union army did not retreat, as it had in so many other battles earlier in the war. Lee, and even some Union soldiers, had expected this to happen again. When a Union soldier in Tennessee heard the news

George wrote many letters to his wife, Margaretta Meade, during the war. On July 3, about four hours before Pickett's Charge, he wrote to tell her about the battle so far. "All [is] well and going on well with the Army. We had a great fight yesterday, the enemy attacking and we completely **repulsing** them; both Armies shattered. To-day at it again, with what result remains to be seen. Army in fine spirits and every one determined to do or die. . . . [General] Reynolds killed the first day. No other of your friends or acquaintances hurt."

George defeated the Confederates at the decisive Battle of Gettysburg in Pennsylvania. The fighting lasted from July 1 to July 3, 1863, during which time a total of 51,000 men were killed or wounded. These battles marked the last time that the South invaded the North.

about Gettysburg, he wrote in his diary, "Well, it was a great wonder that the Army of the Potomac did not fall back."

At nightfall, Lee ordered his men to prepare for marching back to the Potomac River and Virginia. The Confederate commander was upset and blamed himself for the deaths of thousands of men. As the army retreated toward Virginia, Lee told many of his soldiers how sorry he felt about the battle.

After the fighting ended, George wrote to his wife on July 5, 1863, about Gettysburg.

> I think I have written since the battle, but am not sure. It was a grand battle, and is in my judgment a most decided victory, though I did not **annihilate** or [capture] the Confederate Army. This morning [the Confederates] retired in great haste into the mountains, leaving their dead unburied and their wounded on the field . . . . The men behaved splendidly; I really think they are becoming soldiers. They endured long marches, short rations, and stood one of the most terrific cannonadings [bombardments] I ever witnessed.

Gettysburg was the last time the Confederates invaded the North. George had defeated the Confederates in one of the bloodiest battles of the war. But the cost was very high. There were 23,000 Union casualties, and 28,000 Confederates were killed or wounded, making the three days at Gettysburg some of the bloodiest ever seen in North America.

After the battle, with Lee defeated and beginning his retreat, George seemed to be a hero. But this changed shortly after the battle was over.

This meeting of the Union Army of the Potomac included General Ulysses S. Grant (seated in front of trees with legs crossed) and General George Meade (reading a map).

The Road to Virginia

After Pickett's Charge, both armies cared for their wounded men. Ambulances, which were wooden carts pulled by horses, drove across the battlefield looking for injured soldiers. On July 4, Lee and a 17-mile-long Confederate wagon train with thousands of wounded men left Gettysburg for the Potomac River.

George followed behind the Confederates into Maryland. Wherever he went, the people of Maryland treated George like a hero for his victory at Gettysburg. In a July 8 letter to his wife, George wrote about his greeting in Frederick, Maryland. "The people in this place have made a great fuss with me. . . . [S]howers of wreaths and bouquets [are] presented to me, in most complimentary terms. . . . The street has been crowded with people, staring at me."

But while Marylanders treated George well, many leaders in Washington criticized him. They believed he should attack Lee immediately, destroy his army, and end the war. Just days after the battle, George received a telegram from General Halleck, chief general of all Union armies. Halleck was critical of George's decision not to attack Lee. He also told George of President Lincoln's "dissatisfaction" with him. Hurt and angered by this criticism after his great victory, George offered to resign from his job. Seeing how upset George was, Halleck turned down George's resignation. Instead of being fired, George was promoted to the rank of brigadier general.

While in Maryland, Meade continued to be cautious and did not attack the retreating Confederates. He was concerned that his army was exhausted after such a difficult battle and not

These confederate soldiers from Louisiana posed in front of their tent for photographer J.W. Petty.

ready to fight. George also respected Lee as a general. George believed that the Confederates were still powerful, and if attacked, could turn the Union victory at Gettysburg into a defeat.

George decided not to fight any large battles with the enemy. Instead, he used some of his soldiers to **harass** the Confederates as they retreated. There were some skirmishes, or small battles, between Union and Confederate troops during the retreat, but nothing big enough to keep the Southern army from returning home. On July 13, George let Lee's army cross the Potomac River and escape back into Virginia.

Although President Lincoln was very happy with the victory at Gettysburg, he was also angry that George did not destroy the enemy army after Pickett's Charge. Lincoln believed that George should not have let Lee escape to Virginia. The president thought that if George had attacked, he would have easily defeated the Confederates. On July 14, Lincoln even wrote a letter to his commanding general saying how disappointed he was, but never mailed it.

In the letter, President Lincoln said:

> My dear general, I do not believe you appreciate the magnitude of the misfortune involved in Lee's escape. He was within your easy grasp, and to have closed upon him . . . would have ended the war. As it is, the war will be prolonged indefinitely.

At about the same time as the battle in Gettysburg, Union troops commanded by Ulysses S. Grant won a big victory by defeating the Confederates and capturing the important city of Vicksburg, located on the Mississippi River. Lincoln believed that if George had attacked Lee in Maryland, the Confederacy would have been so weakened after its defeats at Vicksburg and Gettysburg, that the government would surrender and end the war.

For the rest of 1863, there were no big battles like Gettysburg. In November 1863, General Grant defeated the Confederates at the Battle of Chattanooga, in southeastern Tennessee.

On November 19, 1863, President Lincoln traveled to Gettysburg. He wanted to see the famous battlefield and to visit the cemetery where Union soldiers were buried. That day, in front of a large crowd of people, Lincoln gave a speech called the Gettysburg Address. His talk lasted less than two minutes, but it is considered one of the most famous speeches in American history. The president hoped that the Civil War would give the United States "a new birth of freedom," freeing all slaves and uniting the North and the South back into one country.

Lincoln was impressed with Grant's victory, and he decided to reward Grant for his success. Lincoln fired General Halleck, and in March 1864 appointed Grant general in chief of all the Union armies, which had about 500,000 soldiers.

As the general in chief, Grant could travel with any division of the Union army. He decided to join George Meade's Army of the Potomac, and fight in Virginia, which Grant believed was the most important state in the Confederacy because the capital city of Richmond was there.

With Grant traveling with the Army of the Potomac, George, the hero of Gettysburg, would no longer be in complete control of his army. He would have to take orders from Grant. George was somewhat disappointed that Grant had chosen his army to travel with, but George told his new boss he would cooperate. Grant appreciated George's comments, and the two generals fought side by side for the rest of the war, with only a few disagreements.

At about the same time Grant became general in chief, the U.S. Congress began an investigation about the Battle of Gettysburg. Many people, including some Union generals, criticized George for not attacking Lee after the battle. They testified to Congress that George should have fought Lee while the Confederates retreated from Gettysburg. Some U.S. Senators also believed George made a mistake and should have battled Lee after Pickett's Charge. George disagreed, and he explained his decisions to Congress.

The investigation ended without Congress saying that George made a mistake. But many people still believed he had. They thought he was too cautious with General Lee. Even President Lincoln felt this way. This was one reason Grant, and not George, became the general in chief. Lincoln believed Grant was the best general in the Union army.

In early spring 1864, Grant created a strategy for ending the war. He ordered General William Tecumseh Sherman, in command of a Union army in southeast Tennessee, to move south into Georgia, attack Atlanta, and then march north into South and North Carolina.

Grant, Meade, and the Army of the Potomac crossed back into Virginia while Sherman invaded

Georgia. Grant knew that after Gettysburg, Lee's army was not strong enough to invade the North again. Instead, Grant wanted to keep the Confederates in Virginia and attack them there. Grant, Lincoln, Meade, and many other Union generals knew that to defeat the South, many more men would be killed and wounded.

For the rest of 1864, the North and South fought many bloody battles. On May 5, both sides fought near Chancellorsville, in the area where they battled in the wilderness nearly one year earlier. This time, Grant had almost 115,000 soldiers, and Lee, about 62,000. After several days of difficult fighting, Grant retreated after the Union suffered nearly 18,000 casualties.

But unlike some past battlefield losses, the Union army did not retreat. Instead, the Army of the Potomac moved to another location and attacked the Confederates again only three days later. After more fighting, the Union lost over 18,000 more soldiers. But the fighting did not stop. In June, Meade and Grant ordered the

Army of the Potomac to attack the enemy near Richmond, and the city of Petersburg, Virginia. Many more Union and Confederate soldiers were killed and wounded in these battles. Both armies seemed to be fighting almost everyday.

These were difficult times for George because so many of his soldiers were being killed or wounded in battle. In just two months, the Union army suffered more than 44,000 casualties. He described how he felt in a June 5, 1864, letter to his wife.

> The sound of the artillery and musketry has just died away. Indeed, we are pretty much engaged [in battle] all the time, from early in the morning till late at night. . . . You would suppose, with all this severe fighting, our severe losses, constant marches, many in the night, that the . . . men would be exhausted . . . but as yet, they show no evidences of it.

These battles hurt Lee's army more than Grant's. Lee had fewer soldiers than the Union did. Losing large numbers of Southern soldiers in fighting meant there were fewer to battle the Army of the Potomac the next time. Also Lee's army was running out of food, medical supplies, and ammunition. Many soldiers also needed

Confederate General Robert E. Lee surrendered the Army of Northern Virginia to Union General Ulysses S. Grant at Appomattox Court House, Virginia. The war that had divided the nation was over.

new shoes and uniforms, but the Confederate army had none to give them.

Fighting continued for the rest of the year. In late 1864 the Union army began a **siege** of Petersburg that lasted many months. The Army of the Potomac surrounded the city, not letting anyone or anything go in or out. Meade and Grant wanted to keep the Confederates from getting any food, water, supplies, or reinforce-ments from outside Petersburg.

By April 1865, Lee knew his soldiers were almost out of food. He had to break out of the city or else his men would starve. On April 2, Lee moved his army out of Petersburg at night. He planned to march west and try to join other Confederate troops. If he could do this, he would have more soldiers to fight the Army of the Potomac.

But Meade and Grant would not let Lee's army escape. They chased the Confederates for almost 90 miles. On April 7 the Army of the Potomac blocked Lee's path near a village in Virginia called Appomattox Court House. The Confederate commander knew that his starving and exhuasted soldiers could not fight anymore. On April 8, General Lee sent a note to General Grant, saying he was ready to give up. The next day, Lee surrendered the Army of Northern Virginia to Grant. The Civil War was over.

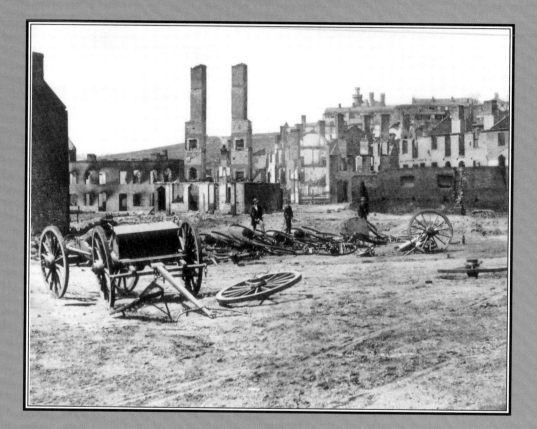

Most of Richmond, Virginia, was ruined. Union forces entered the Confederate capital and found this arsenal and the surrounding neighborhood destroyed by fire.

An American Hero

mericans could not believe the war was finally over. Many changes had happened in the five years since the war began. More than 610,000 soldiers from both sides had been killed during the conflict between the North and South. Over 500,000 soldiers had been wounded. Slaves in the southern states were all free. Large parts of the South, especially in Virginia, had been destroyed by the war. Trees, flowers, and plants of all kinds had been destroyed by the armies during the fighting. Many farmhouses and cities had been ruined.

This 1864 portrait of President Abraham Lincoln was painted by Mathew Brady. John Wilkes Booth, who had supported the Confederacy, shot Lincoln.

But now that all the battles were over, the North and South could unite again and begin to put the country back together.

But on April 15, Americans were shocked and saddened to learn that President Lincoln had been assassinated. He was shot while watching a play with his wife at Ford's Theater in Washington, D.C. John Wilkes Booth, who supported the Confederacy, killed Lincoln because he was angry about the Union's victory in the Civil War.

On June 28, 1865, George Meade's service to the Army of the Potomac ended. After the war, the army gave new assignments to many generals and soldiers. There were no Confederates to fight anymore, but George still had some work to do for the army.

In the spring of 1866, a group of Americans in Cincinnati, Ohio, decided to invade Canada, which was controlled by Great Britain. This group was called the **Fenian Society,** and its members were mostly from Ireland. They wanted Ireland to be independent from Great Britain. The Fenians attacked Canada because their enemy, the British, also ruled Canada.

The U.S. government did not agree with what the Fenians did, and it sent the army to stop them. George commanded the army that was sent to Canada. In June 1866, John O'Neill led about 800 men across the Niagara River near Buffalo in New York State into Canada. They captured Fort Erie, which was a British fort located in Ontario, a province of Canada. Canadian provinces are like American states.

George and his soldiers arrived near Fort Erie shortly after O'Neill did. The large group of U.S. soldiers forced O'Neill to retreat. He ordered his men to return to Buffalo, New York. George followed them back into the United States where O'Neill and about 700 of his men were arrested. George was a hero again.

In August 1866 the U.S. Army gave George another job. He became Commander of the army's Military Division of the Atlantic. This division was located in Philadelphia, Pennsylvania, George's home state. While serving as Commander, George also was Commissioner of

Fairmount Park, a park owned by the City of Philadelphia. As commissioner, George was responsible for keeping the park clean and safe. George enjoyed his time in Philadelphia very much.

By 1868, George left Philadelphia, and from January 1868 to March 1869 he ran the army's Department of the South. But George missed Philadelphia, so the army agreed to send him back and give him his old job as Commander of the Military Division of the Atlantic. He kept this job until he died.

George Gordon Meade died on November 6, 1872, shortly after becoming ill with pneumonia. His doctors believed his war injuries made the pneumonia worse and caused his death.

Although George Meade won the Battle of Gettysburg, the most important fight of the Civil War, some historians still criticize him. They say he was too **cautious** and was afraid of attacking General Lee after the battle. George himself thought he did not get the credit he deserved for

In 1864 the U.S. Congress passed the 13th Amendment and asked each state to approve it. On December 15, 1865, the 13th Amendment to the U.S. Constitution became law. This amendment freed all slaves throughout the United States, in the North and the South, and abolished slavery forever. The amendment ended more than 250 years of slavery for African Americans. President Lincoln supported the amendment in 1864. Unfortunately, he did not live to see the amendment become law at the end of 1865.

his success at Gettysburg. He and many others at the time believed that his victory over Lee was a major factor in the Union's defeat of the Confederacy.

Today, George Meade is remembered as an American hero, who helped bring the country back together. Many monuments honor him across the United States. On March 5, 1929, the U.S. army named a fort in Maryland after the hero of Gettysburg. During World War II, more than three million soldiers were trained at Fort Meade, which is named after one of this country's greatest generals.

GLOSSARY

annihilate–to destroy something.

arsenal–where an army keeps weapons and ammunition.

brigade–a group of soldiers in an army commanded by a colonel or general.

campaign–a series of battles in a war.

cautious–to be very careful.

confederacy–another name for the Confederate States of America; the South.

corps–the largest group of soldiers in the Union or Confederate armies, which was commanded by a general.

courier–a messenger who delivers documents and letters.

division–usually two brigades of soldiers commanded by a general.

Fenian Society–founded in Ireland, with groups also in the United States, its members wanted Ireland to be independent from Great Britain.

general–the highest ranking officer in the army.

harass–to annoy or bother.

rebellion–a violent revolt against a government.

reinforcements–soldiers and equipment used to help the rest of the army.

repulsing–when an army defeats an enemy.

siege–when an army surrounds an enemy town or city.

Seminole War–war fought between the United States and Seminole Indians in Florida.

Union–another name for the Northern United States in the Civil War; the North.

CHRONOLOGY

1815	Born George Gordon Meade on December 31 in Cadiz, Spain.
1831	Enters the United States Military Academy at West Point, New York.
1835	Graduates from West Point and appointed second lieutenant in the U.S. Army.
1836	Sent to Florida to fight in the Seminole War.
1837	Begins to work as railroad surveyor.
1840	Marries Margaretta Sargent.
1842	Designs and builds lighthouses in Delaware.
1846	Goes to Mexico to fight in the Mexican-American War, promoted to first lieutenant.
1856	Promoted to captain
1861	Civil War begins; George promoted to the rank of general in the Union army.
1862	Fights in the Peninsula Campaign, the Second Battle of Bull Run, and the Battles of Antietam and Fredericksburg. Given command of the Fifth Corps.
1863	Appointed commander of the Army of the Potomac by President Abraham Lincoln; defeats Confederate army commanded by Robert E. Lee at the Battle of Gettysburg; promoted to brigadier general

CHRONOLOGY

1864   Fights in the Battle of the Wilderness and the Siege of Petersburg.

1866   Prevents invasion of Canada by Fenian Society.

1866   Becomes commander of the U.S. Army's Military Division of the Atlantic.

1872   Dies on November 6 in Philadelphia, Pennsylvania.

CIVIL WAR TIME LINE ═══════

1860   Abraham Lincoln is elected president of the United States on November 6. During the next few months, Southern states begin to break away from the Union.

1861   On April 12, the Confederates attack Fort Sumter, South Carolina, and the Civil War begins. Union forces are defeated in Virginia at the First Battle of Bull Run (First Manassas) on July 21 and withdraw to Washington, D.C.

1862   Robert E. Lee is placed in command of the main Confederate army in Virginia in June. Lee defeats the Army of the Potomac at the Second Battle of Bull Run (Second Manassas) in Virginia on August 29–30. On September 17, Union general George B. McClellan turns back Lee's first invasion of the North at Antietam Creek near Sharpsburg, Maryland. It is the bloodiest day of the war.

1863   On January 1, President Lincoln issues the Emancipation Proclamation, freeing slaves in Southern states. Between May 1–6, Lee wins an important victory at Chancellorsville, but key Southern commander Thomas J. "Stonewall" Jackson dies from wounds. In June, Union forces hold the city of Vicksburg, Mississippi, under siege. The people of Vicksburg surrender on July 4. Lee's second invasion of the North during July 1–3 is decisively turned back at Gettysburg, Pennsylvania.

1864	General Grant is made supreme Union commander on March 9. Following a series of costly battles, on June 19 Grant successfully encircles Lee's troops in Petersburg, Virginia. A siege of the town lasts nearly a year. Union general William Sherman captures Atlanta on September 2 and begins the "March to the Sea," a campaign of destruction across Georgia and South Carolina. On November 8, Abraham Lincoln wins reelection as president.
1865	On April 2, Petersburg, Virginia, falls to the Union. Lee attempts to reach Confederate forces in North Carolina but is gradually surrounded by Union troops. Lee surrenders to Grant on April 9 at Appomattox, Virginia, ending the war. Abraham Lincoln is assassinated by John Wilkes Booth on April 14.

FURTHER READING

Archer, Jules. *A House Divided: The Lives of Ulysses S. Grant and Robert E. Lee.* New York: Scholastic, 1995.

Beller, Susan Provost. *Never Were Men so Brave–The Irish Brigade During the Civil War.* New York: Simon & Schuster, 1998.

Grabowski, Patricia A. *Robert E. Lee–Confederate General.* Philadelphia: Chelsea House Publishers, 2001.

Lester, Julius. *From Slave Ship to Freedom Road.* New York: Dial Books, 1998.

Murphy, Jim. *The Long Road to Gettysburg.* New York: Clarion Books, 1992.

PICTURE CREDITS

INDEX

ABOUT THE AUTHOR

BRUCE ADELSON has written 12 books for adults and children, including *Brushing Back Jim Crow—The Integration of Minor League Baseball in the American South* and *The Composite Guide to Field Hockey,* as well as three other historical biographies for children. A former elementary school substitute teacher and former commentator for National Public Radio and CBS Radio, Bruce is currently a book/multimedia reviewer for Children's Literature, a practicing attorney, and the proud father of Michael Daniel who was born in April 2001.